EASY VIETNAMESE COOKBOOK

50 AUTHENTIC VIETNAMESE RECIPES

2nd Edition

By
Chef Maggie Chow
Copyright © 2015 by Saxonberg Associates
All rights reserved

Published by
BookSumo, a division of Saxonberg Associates
http://www.booksumo.com/

Stay To the End of the Cookbook and Receive....

I really appreciate when people, take the time to read all of my recipes.

So, as a gift for reading this entire cookbook you will receive a **massive collection of special recipes.**

Read to the end of this cookbook and get my *Easy Specialty Cookbook Box Set for FREE*!

This box set includes the following:

1. *Easy Sushi Cookbook*

2. ***Easy Dump Dinner Cookbook***
3. ***Easy Beans Cookbook***

Remember this box set is about **EASY** cooking.

In the ***Easy Sushi Cookbook*** you will learn the easiest methods to prepare almost every type of Japanese Sushi i.e. *California Rolls, the Perfect Sushi Rice, Crab Rolls, Osaka Style Sushi*, and so many others.

Then we go on to *Dump Dinners*. Nothing can be easier than a Dump Dinner. In the ***Easy Dump Dinner Cookbook*** we will learn how to master our slow cookers and make some amazingly unique dinners that will take almost **no effort**.

Finally in the ***Easy Beans Cookbook*** we tackle one of my favorite side dishes: Beans. There are so many delicious ways to make Baked Beans and Bean Salads that I had to share them.

So stay till the end and then keep on cooking with my *Easy Specialty Cookbook Box Set*!

About the Author.

Maggie Chow is the author and creator of your favorite *Easy Cookbooks* and *The Effortless Chef Series*. Maggie is a lover of all things related to food. Maggie loves nothing more than finding new recipes, trying them out, and then making them her own, by adding or removing ingredients, tweaking cooking times, and anything to make the recipe not only taste better, but be easier to cook!

For a complete listing of all my books please see my author page.

Introduction

Welcome to *The Effortless Chef Series*! Thank you for taking the time to download the *Easy Vietnamese Cookbook*. Come take a journey with me into the delights of easy cooking. The point of this cookbook and all my cookbooks is to exemplify the effortless nature of cooking simply.

In this book we focus on food from the Country of Vietnam. You will find that even though the recipes are simple, the taste of the dishes is quite amazing.

So will you join me in an adventure of simple cooking? If the answer is yes (and I hope it is) please consult the table of contents to find the dishes you are most interested in. Once you are ready jump right in and start cooking.

— Chef Maggie Chow

TABLE OF CONTENTS

STAY TO THE END OF THE COOKBOOK AND RECEIVE.... 2

About the Author.................................. 5

Introduction 7

Table of Contents 8

Legal Notes.. 12

Chapter 1: Easy Vietnamese Recipes .. 13

    Chicken Meatballs In Vietnam 13

    Spring Rolls Vietnamese Style......... 16

    A Vietnamese Inspired Chicken Salad 19

    Lamb Chops In Vietnam 22

    A Southeast Asian Pork I................. 25

    Pho Soup... 28

    Southeast Asian Pork II 31

Easy Vietnamese Inspired Stir-Fry.. 34

Shrimp Soup 38

Chinese Pork Chops 41

Tofu Based Salad In Vietnam 44

Beef and Lettuce 47

Rice-Noodle Salad............................ 50

Chicken Wings in Vietnam.............. 53

Beef Pho... 56

A Chicken & Curry Soup from
Southeast Asia................................. 59

A Vietnamese Condiment................ 62

La Sa Ga 64

(A Vietnamese Soup)....................... 64

Lemon Grass Chicken 67

A Sandwich In Vietnam................... 70

Southeast Asian Pesto Pasta............ 73

Ho Chi Minh City Coffee 76

Bo Nuong Xa.................................... 78

(Mint and Basil Beef) 78

Curry Soup....................................... 81

(Vegetarian Approved).................... 81

Pho III 85

Thit Bo Xao Dau 88

(Bean and Beef Stir Fry) 88

Authentic Vietnamese Vermicelli 91

Bamboo Tofu 95

Radish Mushroom Sandwich 99

Nem Ran Hay Cha Gio 103

(Vietnamese Spring Rolls) 103

Southeast Asian Chicken Breasts .. 106

Chicken and Rice Soup 109

Shrimp Cucumber Sandwich 112

Nuoc Cham 115

(Vietnamese Beef Sauce) 115

Bo Luc Lac with Asian Vinaigrette 117

(Garlic Sirloin) 117

Bo Luc Lac II 121

(Garlic Tenderloin) 121

Lemongrass Chicken 125

Vietnamese Spring Rolls 128

Rice and Shrimp Salad 131

Pho IV 134

Lime Cilantro Catfish 138

Vietnamese Green Beans............... 141

Hanoi Rice Noodle Spicy Salad 144

A Vietnamese Drink 148

Lemon Cabbage Lunch Vietnamese Style 151

THANKS FOR READING! NOW LET'S TRY SOME **SUSHI** AND **DUMP DINNERS**....
.... 154

Come On... 156

Let's Be Friends :)........................... 156

Can I Ask A Favour? 157

Interested in Other Easy Cookbooks?
.... 158

Legal Notes

ALL RIGHTS RESERVED. NO PART OF THIS BOOK MAY BE REPRODUCED OR TRANSMITTED IN ANY FORM OR BY ANY MEANS. PHOTOCOPYING, POSTING ONLINE, AND / OR DIGITAL COPYING IS STRICTLY PROHIBITED UNLESS WRITTEN PERMISSION IS GRANTED BY THE BOOK'S PUBLISHING COMPANY. LIMITED USE OF THE BOOK'S TEXT IS PERMITTED FOR USE IN REVIEWS WRITTEN FOR THE PUBLIC AND/OR PUBLIC DOMAIN.

Chapter 1: Easy Vietnamese Recipes

Chicken Meatballs In Vietnam

Ingredients

- 1 1/2 pounds ground chicken
- 1 clove garlic, minced
- 1 egg white
- 1 tbsp rice wine
- 2 tbsps soy sauce
- 1/2 tsp Worcestershire sauce
- 2 tsps fish sauce
- 1/2 tsp white sugar
- salt and white pepper to taste
- 2 tbsps cornstarch
- 1 tbsp sesame oil

Directions

- Preheat the broiler of your oven before doing anything else.
- Combine ground chicken, Worcestershire sauce, sugar, garlic, rice wine, soy sauce, egg white, fish sauce, salt, pepper, corn starch and sesame oil in a medium sized bowl before forming small balls out of it and threading them onto skewers.
- Put these skewers on a baking sheet.
- Broil it for 20 minutes or until you see that it is cooked.

Serving: 6

Timing Information:

Preparation	Cooking	Total Time
20 mins	35 mins	55 mins

Nutritional Information:

Calories	184 kcal
Carbohydrates	4.1 g
Cholesterol	69 mg
Fat	5.9 g
Fiber	0.1 g
Protein	26.5 g
Sodium	497 mg

* Percent Daily Values are based on a 2,000 calorie diet.

Spring Rolls Vietnamese Style

Ingredients

- 2 ounces rice vermicelli
- 8 rice wrappers (8.5 inch diameter)
- 8 large cooked shrimp - peeled, deveined and cut in half
- 1 1/3 tbsps chopped fresh Thai basil
- 3 tbsps chopped fresh mint leaves
- 3 tbsps chopped fresh cilantro
- 2 leaves lettuce, chopped
- 4 tsps fish sauce
- 1/4 cup water
- 2 tbsps fresh lime juice
- 1 clove garlic, minced
- 2 tbsps white sugar
- 1/2 tsp garlic chili sauce
- 3 tbsps hoisin sauce
- 1 tsp finely chopped peanuts

Directions

- Cook rice vermicelli in boiling water for five minutes or until done and then drain.
- Dip a rice wrapper in hot water for one second to soften it up before placing shrimp halves, basil, mint, vermicelli, cilantro and lettuce, and then roll this wrapper around these things.
- Mix fish sauce, lime juice, garlic, water, sugar and chili sauce in a small bowl before mixing peanuts and hoisin sauce in a separate bowl.
- Serve spring roll with these two sauces.

Serving: 8

Timing Information:

Preparation	Cooking	Total Time
45 mins	5 mins	50 mins

Nutritional Information:

Calories	82 kcal
Carbohydrates	15.8 g
Cholesterol	11 mg
Fat	0.7 g
Fiber	0.6 g
Protein	3.3 g
Sodium	305 mg

* Percent Daily Values are based on a 2,000 calorie diet.

A Vietnamese Inspired Chicken Salad

Ingredients

- 1 tbsp finely chopped green chile peppers
- 1 tbsp rice vinegar
- 2 tbsps fresh lime juice
- 3 tbsps Asian fish sauce
- 3 cloves garlic, minced
- 1 tbsp white sugar
- 1 tbsp Asian (toasted) sesame oil
- 2 tbsps vegetable oil
- 1 tsp black pepper
- 2 cooked skinless boneless chicken breast halves, shredded
- 1/2 head cabbage, cored and thinly sliced
- 1 carrot, cut into matchsticks
- 1/3 onion, finely chopped
- 1/3 cup finely chopped dry roasted peanuts
- 1/3 cup chopped fresh cilantro

Directions

- Combine chopped green chilies, sesame oil, lime juice, fish sauce, garlic, sugar, rice vinegar, vegetable oil and black pepper in a medium sized bowl very thoroughly so that the sugar is completely dissolved.
- Mix chicken, carrot, onion, peanuts, cabbage and cilantro in a separate bowl.
- Pour the bowl containing dressing over this and serve it after thoroughly mixing it.

Serving: 4

Timing Information:

Preparation	Cooking	Total Time
30 mins		30 mins

Nutritional Information:

Calories	303 kcal
Carbohydrates	19.3 g
Cholesterol	37 mg
Fat	17.9 g
Fiber	5.7 g
Protein	19.2 g
Sodium	991 mg

* Percent Daily Values are based on a 2,000 calorie diet.

Lamb Chops In Vietnam

Ingredients

- 15 (3 ounce) lamb loin chops (1-inch thick) lamb loin chops (1-inch thick)
- 2 cloves garlic, sliced
- 1 tsp garlic powder, or to taste
- 1 pinch chili powder
- 2 tbsps white sugar
- freshly ground black pepper to taste
- 1 tbsp fresh lime juice
- 1 tbsp soy sauce
- 2 tbsps olive oil
- 1/4 cup chopped fresh cilantro
- 2 lime wedges
- 2 lemon wedges

Directions

- Set your oven at 400 degrees F before doing anything else.
- Add the garlic, garlic powder, sugar, salt, lime juice, chili

powder, soy sauce, olive oil and pepper in a roasting pan over lamb chops.
- Bake this in the preheated oven for about 30 minutes or until tender before garnishing it with cilantro and adding some lime juice.
- Serve.

Serving: 5

Timing Information:

Preparation	Cooking	Total Time
10 mins	20 mins	8 hr 30 mins

Nutritional Information:

Calories	555 kcal
Carbohydrates	7.4 g
Cholesterol	151 mg
Fat	40.4 g
Fiber	0.6 g
Protein	38.6 g
Sodium	301 mg

* Percent Daily Values are based on a 2,000 calorie diet.

A Southeast Asian Pork I

Ingredients

- 1 tbsp vegetable oil
- 1 cup white sugar
- 2 pounds pork spareribs, cut into 1-inch pieces
- 2 green onions, cut in 2-inch lengths
- 1 green chili pepper, chopped
- 1 tsp ground black pepper
- 2 shallots, finely chopped
- 2 cloves garlic, minced
- salt to taste
- 1 tsp Asian (toasted) sesame oil
- 1 tbsp green onion, thinly sliced and separated into rings

Directions

- Cook sugar in hot oil in a skillet until you see that it is turning brown in color before adding pork, 2 green onions, black pepper, chili pepper, shallots,

garlic, and salt, and mixing all this very thoroughly in the caramelized sugar.
- After the pork turns golden brown; add sesame oil and vegetables into it before turning down the heat to low and cooking it for a few minutes.
- When you see that juices have been absorbed then turn up the heat to high and cook all this for five minutes or until you see that the sauce is thick enough.
- Garnish this with some green onion rings.
- Serve

Serving: 4

Timing Information:

Preparation	Cooking	Total Time
15 mins	20 mins	35 mins

Nutritional Information:

Calories	657 kcal
Carbohydrates	56.8 g
Cholesterol	120 mg
Fat	34.7 g
Fiber	0.7 g
Protein	29.9 g
Sodium	98 mg

* Percent Daily Values are based on a 2,000 calorie diet.

Pho Soup

Ingredients

- 2 (14.5 ounce) cans chicken broth
- 2 star anise pods, or more to taste
- 3/4 tbsp ginger paste
- 1 tsp sriracha hot sauce, or more to taste
- 4 ounces tofu, cubed
- 1/2 cup broccoli florets
- 1/2 cup sliced mushrooms
- 1/4 cup chopped carrots
- 1/2 (8 ounce) package dried thin rice noodles
- 1 tbsp chopped green onion

Directions

- Bring the mixture of chicken broth, ginger paste, star anise and sriracha hot sauce to boil before adding carrots, tofu, mushrooms and broccoli, and cooking it for seven minutes or until you see that the vegetables are tender.

- Put noodles in hot water for about four minutes and drain.
- After removing star anise from the broth mixture, add this mixture on top of noodles in serving bowls.
- Serve.

Serving: 4

Timing Information:

Preparation	Cooking	Total Time
15 mins	10 mins	25 mins

Nutritional Information:

Calories	159 kcal
Carbohydrates	29.2 g
Cholesterol	5 mg
Fat	2.3 g
Fiber	1.7 g
Protein	5.2 g
Sodium	991 mg

* Percent Daily Values are based on a 2,000 calorie diet.

Southeast Asian Pork II

Ingredients

- 4 pounds pork shoulder, cut into cubes
- 1 tsp salt
- 1 tsp ground black pepper
- 1/4 cup olive oil
- 2 cloves garlic, minced
- 2 tbsps brown sugar
- 2 tbsps soy sauce
- 1 tbsp fish sauce
- 1 tsp Chinese five-spice powder

Directions

- Cook garlic and pork that is seasoned with salt and pepper in hot oil for about ten minutes or until you see that pork is browned.
- Now add brown sugar, five-spice powder, soy sauce and fish sauce into the pork before turning down the heat to low and cooking it for

2 full hours or until you see that pork is tender.
- Serve.

Serving: 4

Timing Information:

Preparation	Cooking	Total Time
10 mins	2 hr 20 mins	2 hr 30 mins

Nutritional Information:

Calories	288 kcal
Carbohydrates	4.4 g
Cholesterol	85 mg
Fat	16.4 g
Fiber	0.1 g
Protein	29.5
Sodium	713 mg

* Percent Daily Values are based on a 2,000 calorie diet.

Easy Vietnamese Inspired Stir-Fry

Ingredients

- 1/4 cup olive oil
- 4 cloves garlic, minced
- 1 (1 inch) piece fresh ginger root, minced
- 1/4 cup fish sauce
- 1/4 cup reduced-sodium soy sauce
- 1 dash sesame oil
- 2 pounds sirloin tip, thinly sliced
- 1 tbsp vegetable oil
- 2 cloves garlic, minced
- 3 green onions, cut into 2 inch pieces
- 1 large onion, thinly sliced
- 2 cups frozen whole green beans, partially thawed
- 1/2 cup reduced-sodium beef broth
- 2 tbsps lime juice
- 1 tbsp chopped fresh Thai basil

- 1 tbsp chopped fresh mint
- 1 pinch red pepper flakes, or to taste
- 1/2 tsp ground black pepper
- 1/4 cup chopped fresh cilantro

Directions

- Add a mixture of olive oil, ginger, fish sauce, 4 cloves of garlic, soy sauce, and sesame oil into a plastic bag containing beef sirloin tips and shake it well to get beef coated with the mixture.
- Refrigerate it for at least two straight hours before removing the beef from the marinade.
- Cook this beef in hot oil for about seven minutes or until you see that it is no longer pink before setting it aside on a plate.
- Turn down the heat to medium and cook garlic, onion and green onion for about five minutes before adding green beans, lime juice, basil, mint, beef broth, red

pepper flakes, pepper and also the beef.
- Mix it thoroughly before adding cilantro.

Serving: 5

Timing Information:

Preparation	Cooking	Total Time
20 mins	30 mins	2 hr 50 mins

Nutritional Information:

Calories	475 kcal
Carbohydrates	8.8 g
Cholesterol	101 mg
Fat	34.4 g
Fiber	2 g
Protein	31.7 g
Sodium	1174 mg

* Percent Daily Values are based on a 2,000 calorie diet.

Shrimp Soup

Ingredients

- 1 tbsp vegetable oil
- 2 tsps minced fresh garlic
- 2 tsps minced fresh ginger root
- 1 (10 ounce) package frozen chopped spinach, thawed and drained
- salt and black pepper to taste
- 2 quarts chicken stock
- 1 cup shrimp stock
- 1 tsp hot pepper sauce(optional)
- 1 tsp hoisin sauce(optional)
- 20 peeled and deveined medium shrimp
- 1 (6.75 ounce) package long rice noodles (rice vermicelli)
- 2 green onions, chopped(optional)

Directions

- Cook garlic and ginger for about one minute before adding

spinach, pepper and salt, and cooking it for 3 more minutes to get the spinach tender.
- Add chicken stock, hoisin sauce, shrimp stock and hot pepper sauce, and cook this for a few more minutes.
- In the end, add noodles and shrimp into it, and cook it for 4 minutes before adding green onions cooking it for another five minutes.
- Add salt and pepper according to your taste before serving.
- Enjoy.

Serving: 6

Timing Information:

Preparation	Cooking	Total Time
15 mins	20 mins	40 mins

Nutritional Information:

Calories	212 kcal
Carbohydrates	28.6 g
Cholesterol	52 mg
Fat	4.7 g
Fiber	2.7 g
Protein	14.4 g
Sodium	1156 mg

* Percent Daily Values are based on a 2,000 calorie diet.

Chinese Pork Chops

Ingredients

- 2 tbsps brown sugar
- 2 tbsps honey
- 2 tbsps fish sauce
- 3 tbsps vegetable oil
- 2 tbsps soy sauce
- 1/2 tsp Worcestershire sauce
- 1/2 tsp minced fresh ginger root
- 1 tsp Chinese five-spice powder
- 1 tsp sesame oil
- 1 tsp minced shallot
- 6 cloves garlic, minced
- 1/2 onion, chopped
- 2 lemon grass, chopped
- 1/4 tsp salt
- 1/2 tsp ground black pepper
- 6 thin, boneless center-cut pork chops
- 1/4 cup vegetable oil

Directions

- Add the mixture brown sugar, honey, lemon grass, soy sauce, Worcestershire sauce, ginger, five-spice powder, sesame oil, fish sauce, shallot, garlic, onion, vegetable oil, salt, and pepper into a plastic bag containing pork chops, and mix it well to coat pork chops thoroughly before refrigerating it for at least eight hours.
- Cook these pork chops on a preheated grill that is lightly oiled for about four minutes each side.
- Serve.

Serving: 6

Timing Information:

Preparation	Cooking	Total Time
15 mins	10 mins	8 hr 25 mins

Nutritional Information:

Calories	416 kcal
Carbohydrates	15 g
Cholesterol	63 mg
Fat	28.8 g
Fiber	0.3 g
Protein	24.5 g
Sodium	814 mg

* Percent Daily Values are based on a 2,000 calorie diet.

Tofu Based Salad In Vietnam

Ingredients

- 1 tbsp vegetable oil
- 2 tbsps chopped garlic
- 1 (14 ounce) package tofu, drained and cubed
- 1/2 cup peanuts
- 2 tbsps soy sauce
- 2 large cucumbers, peeled and thinly sliced
- 1/2 cup Vietnamese sweet chili sauce
- 1/4 cup lime juice
- 1 bunch chopped cilantro leaves

Directions

- Cook garlic in hot oil for about thirty seconds before adding tofu and peanuts, and cooking it again until tofu is lightly brown.
- Now add soy sauce and cook until you see that it is completely

absorbed before refrigerating it for at least one hour.
- In the mixture of chili sauce, cilantro, sliced cucumbers and lime juice add tofu, and mix it thoroughly before serving.
- Enjoy.

Serving: 6

Timing Information:

Preparation	Cooking	Total Time
15 mins	25 mins	1 hr 40 mins

Nutritional Information:

Calories	200 kcal
Carbohydrates	18.4 g
Cholesterol	0 mg
Fat	11.7 g
Fiber	2.6 g
Protein	9.5 g
Sodium	636 mg

* Percent Daily Values are based on a 2,000 calorie diet.

BEEF AND LETTUCE

Ingredients

- 1 cup uncooked long grain white rice
- 2 cups water
- 5 tsps white sugar
- 1 clove garlic, minced
- 1/4 cup fish sauce
- 5 tbsps water
- 1 1/2 tbsps chili sauce
- 1 lemon, juiced
- 2 tbsps vegetable oil
- 3 cloves garlic, minced
- 1 pound ground beef
- 1 tbsp ground cumin
- 1 (28 ounce) can canned diced tomatoes
- 2 cups lettuce leaves, torn into 1/2 inch wide strips

Directions

- Bring the water containing rice to boil before turning down the heat

to low and cooking for 25 minutes.
- Add mashed sugar and garlic to the mixture of chili sauce, fish sauce, lemon juice and water in a medium sized bowl.
- Cook garlic in hot oil before adding beef and cumin, and cooking all this until you see that it is brown.
- Now add half of that fish sauce mixture and tomatoes into the pan, and after turning down the heat to low, cook all this for twenty more minutes.
- Add lettuce into this beef mixture before serving this over the cooked rice along with that remaining fish sauce.

Serving: 6

Timing Information:

Preparation	Cooking	Total Time
15 mins	45 mins	1 hr

Nutritional Information:

Calories	529 kcal
Carbohydrates	56.9 g
Cholesterol	69 mg
Fat	21 g
Fiber	4 g
Protein	26.3 g
Sodium	1481 mg

* Percent Daily Values are based on a 2,000 calorie diet.

Rice-Noodle Salad

Ingredients

- 5 cloves garlic
- 1 cup loosely packed chopped cilantro
- 1/2 jalapeno pepper, seeded and minced
- 3 tbsps white sugar
- 1/4 cup fresh lime juice
- 3 tbsps vegetarian fish sauce
- 1 (12 ounce) package dried rice noodles
- 2 carrots, julienned
- 1 cucumber, halved lengthwise and chopped
- 1/4 cup chopped fresh mint
- 4 leaves napa cabbage
- 1/4 cup unsalted peanuts
- 4 sprigs fresh mint

Directions

- Add a mashed mixture of hot pepper, garlic and cilantro into

the bowl containing mixture of lime juice, sugar and fish sauce before letting it stand for at least five minutes.
- Cook rice noodles in boiling salty water for two minutes before draining it and passing it through cold water to stop the process of cooking.
- Mix sauce, carrots, cucumber, noodles, mint and Napa in large sized serving bowl very thoroughly before garnishing it with peanuts and mint sprigs.

Serving: 4

Timing Information:

Preparation	Cooking	Total Time
15 mins		15 mins

Nutritional Information:

Calories	432 kcal
Carbohydrates	89.5 g
Cholesterol	0 mg
Fat	5.3 g
Fiber	4.1 g
Protein	6.6 g
Sodium	188 mg

* Percent Daily Values are based on a 2,000 calorie diet.

Chicken Wings in Vietnam

Ingredients

- 12 chicken wings, tips removed and wings cut in half at joint
- 2 cloves garlic, peeled and coarsely chopped
- 1/2 onion, cut into chunks
- 1/4 cup soy sauce
- 1/4 cup Asian fish sauce
- 2 tbsps fresh lemon juice
- 2 tbsps sesame oil
- 1 tsp salt
- 1 tsp freshly ground black pepper
- 1 tbsp garlic powder
- 1 tbsp white sugar

Directions

- Into the mixture of chicken wings, onion and garlic in large sized bowl; add fish sauce, sesame oi, salt, sugar, garlic powder, pepper and lemon juice

before refrigerating it covered for at least two hours.
- Preheat your oven at 400 degrees F and place aluminum foil in the baking dish.
- Reserving some marinade for brushing; place all the wings on the baking dish and bake it for about 30 minutes or until you see that these have turned golden brown.

Serving: 4

Timing Information:

Preparation	Cooking	Total Time
15 mins	30 mins	2 hr 45 mins

Nutritional Information:

Calories	716 kcal
Carbohydrates	9.1 g
Cholesterol	213 mg
Fat	50.9 g
Fiber	0.8 g
Protein	53 g
Sodium	2781 mg

* Percent Daily Values are based on a 2,000 calorie diet.

Beef Pho

Ingredients

- 4 quarts beef broth
- 1 large onion, sliced into rings
- 6 slices fresh ginger root
- 1 lemon grass
- 1 cinnamon stick
- 1 tsp whole black peppercorns
- 1 pound sirloin tip, cut into thin slices
- 1/2 pound bean sprouts
- 1 cup fresh basil leaves
- 1 cup fresh mint leaves
- 1 cup loosely packed cilantro leaves
- 3 fresh jalapeno peppers, sliced into rings
- 2 limes, cut into wedges
- 2 (8 ounce) packages dried rice noodles
- 1/2 tbsp hoisin sauce
- 1 dash hot pepper sauce
- 3 tbsps fish sauce

Directions

- Bring the mixture of broth, onion, lemon grass, cinnamon, ginger and peppercorns to boil before turning down the heat to low and cooking it for about one hour.
- Place bean sprouts, basil, cilantro, chilies, mint and lime on a platter very neatly.
- Place noodles in hot water for about 15 minutes before placing it in six different bowls evenly.
- Put raw beef over it before pouring in hot broth.
- Serve it with the platter and sauces.

Serving: 6

Timing Information:

Preparation	Cooking	Total Time
10 mins	1 hr 20 mins	1 hr 30 mins

Nutritional Information:

Calories	528 kcal
Carbohydrates	73.1 g
Cholesterol	51 mg
Fat	13.6 g
Fiber	3.9 g
Protein	27.1 g
Sodium	2844 mg

* Percent Daily Values are based on a 2,000 calorie diet.

A Chicken & Curry Soup from Southeast Asia

Ingredients

- 2 tbsps vegetable oil
- 1 (3 pound) whole chicken, skin removed and cut into pieces
- 1 onion, cut into chunks
- 2 shallots, thinly sliced
- 2 cloves garlic, chopped
- 1/8 cup thinly sliced fresh ginger root
- 1 stalk lemon grass, cut into 2 inch pieces
- 4 tbsps curry powder
- 1 green bell pepper, cut into 1 inch pieces
- 2 carrots, sliced diagonally
- 1 quart chicken broth
- 1 quart water
- 2 tbsps fish sauce
- 2 kaffir lime leaves
- 1 bay leaf

- 2 tsps red pepper flakes
- 8 small potatoes, quartered
- 1 (14 ounce) can coconut milk
- 1 bunch fresh cilantro

Directions

- Cook onion and chicken in hot oil until you see that onions are soft and then set it aside for later use.
- Cook shallots in the same pan for one minute before adding garlic, lemon grass, ginger and curry powder, and cooking it for another five minutes.
- Add pepper and carrots before stirring in chicken, onion, fish sauce, chicken broth and water.
- Also add lime leaves, red pepper flakes and bay leaf before bringing all this to boil and adding potatoes.
- Add coconut milk and cook it for 60 minutes after turning down the heat to low.
- Garnish with a sprig of fresh cilantro.
- Serve.

Serving: 8

Timing Information:

Preparation	Cooking	Total Time
30 mins	2 hr	2 hr 30 mins

Nutritional Information:

Calories	512 kcal
Carbohydrates	40.6 g
Cholesterol	75 mg
Fat	26.8 g
Fiber	6.7 g
Protein	29.8 g
Sodium	374 mg

* Percent Daily Values are based on a 2,000 calorie diet.

A Vietnamese Condiment

Ingredients

- 1/4 cup white sugar
- 1/2 cup warm water
- 1/4 cup fish sauce
- 1/3 cup distilled white vinegar
- 1/2 lemon, juiced
- 3 cloves garlic, minced
- 3 Thai chile peppers, chopped
- 1 green onion, thinly sliced

Directions

- In a mixture of warm water and sugar; add fish sauce, garlic, green onion, lemon juice, vinegar and chili pepper.
- Mix all this very thoroughly before serving.
- Enjoy.

NOTE: Use this condiment for dipping spring rolls in, or as a topping for jasmine rice.

Serving: 5

Timing Information:

Preparation	Cooking	Total Time
15 mins		15 mins

Nutritional Information:

Calories	15 kcal
Carbohydrates	3.7 g
Cholesterol	0 mg
Fat	0 g
Fiber	0.3 g
Protein	0.4 g
Sodium	220 mg

* Percent Daily Values are based on a 2,000 calorie diet.

La Sa Ga

(A Vietnamese Soup)

Ingredients

- 3 tbsps peanut oil
- 1 cup diced onion
- 3 tbsps minced garlic
- 1 cup coconut milk, divided
- 1 tbsp red curry paste, or more to taste
- 2 cooked chicken breast halves, shredded
- 8 cups chicken stock
- 6 tbsps soy sauce, or to taste
- 1/4 cup fish sauce, or to taste
- 1 1/2 pounds angel hair pasta
- 1/4 cup chopped fresh basil, or to taste

Directions

- Cook onion and garlic in hot oil for about four minutes before adding

coconut milk and stirring it continuously for about two minutes.
- Now add curry paste and stir it well for about two more minutes.
- Introduce chicken stock into the pan and cook it for about four minutes after turning up the heat to medium.
- Cook it for another four minutes after adding the remaining coconut milk.
- Stir in angel hair pasta before covering up the pot and cooking it for ten more minutes.
- Add basil before serving.

Serving: 8

Timing Information:

Preparation	Cooking	Total Time
20 mins	20 mins	40 mins

Nutritional Information:

Calories	333 kcal
Carbohydrates	41.8 g
Cholesterol	15 mg
Fat	13.5 g
Fiber	3.1 g
Protein	15.1 g
Sodium	1710 mg

* Percent Daily Values are based on a 2,000 calorie diet.

Lemon Grass Chicken

Ingredients

- 2 tbsps vegetable oil
- 1 lemon grass, minced
- 1 (3 pound) whole chicken, cut into pieces
- 2/3 cup water
- 1 tbsp fish sauce
- 1 1/2 tbsps curry powder
- 1 tbsp cornstarch
- 1 tbsp chopped cilantro(optional)

Directions

- Cook lemon grass in hot oil for about 5 minutes before adding chicken and cooking it until you see that the chicken is no longer pink from the center.
- Now add fish sauce, curry powder and water into the pan before turning the heat up to high and cooking it for another 15 minutes.

- Now add the mixture of curry sauce and cornstarch into the pan, and cook all this for another five minutes.
- Garnish with cilantro before serving.

Serving: 4

Timing Information:

Preparation	Cooking	Total Time
15 mins	25 mins	40 mins

Nutritional Information:

Calories	813 kcal
Carbohydrates	4.6 g
Cholesterol	255 mg
Fat	58.4 g
Fiber	0.8 g
Protein	63.8 g
Sodium	515 mg

* Percent Daily Values are based on a 2,000 calorie diet.

A Sandwich In Vietnam

Ingredients

- 4 boneless pork loin chops, cut 1/4 inch thick
- 4 (7 inch) French bread baguettes, split lengthwise
- 4 tsps mayonnaise, or to taste
- 1 ounce chili sauce with garlic
- 1/4 cup fresh lime juice
- 1 small red onion, sliced into rings
- 1 medium cucumber, peeled and sliced lengthwise
- 2 tbsps chopped fresh cilantro
- salt and pepper to taste

Directions

- Put pork chops on the broiling pan and cook it for about 5 minutes or until you see that it is brown from each side.
- Put mayonnaise evenly on French rolls and also put one pork chop on each roll.

- Put chili sauce on the meat and add some lime juice, while topping it with onion, pepper, cucumber, salt and cilantro.
- Add some more lime juice just before serving.

Serving: 4

Timing Information:

Preparation	Cooking	Total Time
10 mins	5 mins	15 mins

Nutritional Information:

Calories	627 kcal
Carbohydrates	72.1 g
Cholesterol	124 mg
Fat	12.1 g
Fiber	3.3 g
Protein	55.3 g
Sodium	1005 mg

* Percent Daily Values are based on a 2,000 calorie diet.

Southeast Asian Pesto Pasta

Ingredients

- 1 lb dried rice noodles
- 1 1/2 C. chopped fresh cilantro
- 1/2 C. sweet Thai basil
- 2 cloves garlic, halved
- 1/2 tsp minced lemon grass bulb
- 1 jalapeno pepper, seeded and minced
- 1 tbsp vegetarian fish sauce
- 4 tbsps chopped, unsalted dry-roasted peanuts
- 7 tbsps canola oil
- 1/2 lime, cut into wedges
- salt and pepper to taste

Directions

- Let your noodles sit submerged in water for 40 mins then remove all the liquids.

- Add the following to the bowl of food processor and begin to puree: 2 tbsps peanuts, cilantro, fish sauce, basil, jalapenos, garlic cloves, and lemongrass.
- Now add in your oil and continue pulsing for a min then add the rest of the peanuts.
- Now heat your noodles in 1/2 C. of water until all the water has been absorbed by the noodles.
- Pour in your most of basil puree then stir everything. Taste the mix then add the rest of the puree if you prefer.
- Top the pasta with 2 more tbsp of peanuts.
- Enjoy.

Serving: 4

Timing Information:

Preparation	Cooking	Total Time
30 m	5 m	35 m

Nutritional Information:

Calories	694 kcal
Fat	29.8 g
Carbohydrates	98.8g
Protein	6.8 g
Cholesterol	0 mg
Sodium	217 mg

* Percent Daily Values are based on a 2,000 calorie diet.

Ho Chi Minh City Coffee

Ingredients

- 4 C. water
- 1/2 C. dark roast ground coffee beans
- 1/2 C. sweetened condensed milk
- 16 ice cubes

Directions

- Make your coffee with the 4 C. of fresh water. Then add 2 tbsps of condensed milk.
- Serve the coffee hot and pour it over 4 ices cubes in a glass.
- Enjoy.

Serving: 4

Timing Information:

Preparation	Cooking	Total Time
5 m	5 m	10 m

Nutritional Information:

Calories	129 kcal
Fat	3.3 g
Carbohydrates	22g
Protein	3.3 g
Cholesterol	13 mg
Sodium	64 mg

* Percent Daily Values are based on a 2,000 calorie diet.

Bo Nuong Xa

(Mint and Basil Beef)

Ingredients

- 2 tsps white sugar
- 2 tbsps soy sauce
- 1 tsp ground black pepper
- 2 cloves garlic, minced
- 2 stalks lemon grass, minced
- 2 tsps sesame seeds
- 1 1/2 lbs sirloin tip, thinly sliced
- skewers
- 12 leaves romaine lettuce
- fresh cilantro for garnish
- fresh basil for garnish
- fresh mint for garnish
- thinly sliced green onion for garnish

Directions

- Get a bowl, combine: sesame seeds, sugar, lemon grass, soy sauce, garlic, and pepper. Add in the meat and stir the mix.
- Place a covering of plastic on the bowl and put everything in the fridge for 5 hrs.
- Now get your grill hot and stake your meat onto the skewers. Grill the kebabs for 6 mins per side.
- When serving the dish place the meat on some fresh lettuce leaves then top everything with green onions, cilantro, basil, and mint.
- Enjoy.

Serving: 6

Timing Information:

Preparation	Cooking	Total Time
20 m	10 m	4 h 30 m

Nutritional Information:

Calories	204 kcal
Fat	11.1 g
Carbohydrates	5.7g
Protein	20.1 g
Cholesterol	61 mg
Sodium	348 mg

* Percent Daily Values are based on a 2,000 calorie diet.

Curry Soup

(Vegetarian Approved)

Ingredients

- 2 tbsps vegetable oil
- 1 onion, coarsely chopped
- 2 shallots, thinly sliced
- 2 cloves garlic, chopped
- 2 inch piece fresh ginger root, thinly sliced
- 1 stalk lemon grass, cut into 2 inch pieces
- 4 tbsps curry powder
- 1 green bell pepper, coarsely chopped
- 2 carrots, peeled and diagonally sliced
- 8 mushrooms, sliced
- 1 lb fried tofu, cut into bite-size pieces
- 4 C. vegetable broth
- 4 C. water

- 2 tbsps vegetarian fish sauce (optional)
- 2 tsps red pepper flakes
- 1 bay leaf
- 2 kaffir lime leaves
- 8 small potatoes, quartered
- 1 (14 oz.) can coconut milk
- 2 C. fresh bean sprouts, for garnish
- 8 sprigs fresh chopped cilantro, for garnish

Directions

- Stir fry your shallots and onions in oil until the onions are see through then add in the curry powder, garlic, lemon grass, and ginger.
- Let the mix continue to fry for 6 mins then add the tofu, green pepper, mushrooms, and carrots.
- Stir the mix then add in the water, pepper flakes, fish sauce, and veggie stock.

- Get everything boiling then add the coconut milk and the potatoes.
- Get the mix boiling again then set the heat to low and let the mix gently boil for 50 mins.
- When serving the dish top each serving with cilantro and bean sprouts.
- Enjoy.

Serving: 8

Timing Information:

Preparation	Cooking	Total Time
30 m	1 h 30 m	2 h

Nutritional Information:

Calories	479 kcal
Fat	26.5 g
Carbohydrates	51.4g
Protein	16.4 g
Cholesterol	0 mg
Sodium	271 mg

* Percent Daily Values are based on a 2,000 calorie diet.

Pho III

Ingredients

- 4 oz. dry Chinese egg noodles
- 6 C. chicken stock
- 2 tbsps fish sauce
- 4 cloves garlic, minced
- 2 tsps minced fresh ginger root
- 1 tbsp minced lemon grass
- 5 green onions, chopped
- 2 C. cubed cooked chicken
- 1 C. bean sprouts
- 1 C. chopped bok choy

Directions

- Get a big pot of water boiling then combine in the noodles and cook them for 9 mins. Then remove the liquids and place the noodles to the side.
- Now add the following to the same pot and get it all boiling

again: green onions, chickens tock, lemon grass, fish sauce, ginger, and garlic.
- Once the mix is boiling set the heat to low and let everything gently cook for 12 mins.
- Combine in the bok choy, bean sprouts, and chicken.
- Continue simmering the mix for 7 mins.
- Divide the noodles into two bowls for serving then top them liberally with the soup.
- Enjoy.

Serving: 2

Timing Information:

Preparation	Cooking	Total Time
10 m	30 m	40 m

Nutritional Information:

Calories	521 kcal
Fat	13.7 g
Carbohydrates	54.4g
Protein	49.8 g
Cholesterol	1107 mg
Sodium	3270 mg

* Percent Daily Values are based on a 2,000 calorie diet.

Thit Bo Xao Dau

(Bean and Beef Stir Fry)

Ingredients

- 1 clove garlic, minced
- 1/4 tsp ground black pepper
- 1 tsp cornstarch
- 1 tsp vegetable oil
- 1 lb sirloin tips, thinly sliced
- 3 tbsps vegetable oil
- 1/2 onion, thinly sliced
- 2 C. fresh green beans, washed and trimmed
- 1/4 C. chicken broth
- 1 tsp soy sauce

Directions

- Get a bowl, combine: 1 tsp veggie oil, garlic, cornstarch, and black pepper. Combine in the beef then stir the mix again.

- Add 2 more tsp of oil to a wok and get it hot. Once the oil is hot begin to stir the meat for 3 mins then place the meat to the side.
- Add 1 more tsp to the wok and being to stir your onions until they are soft then add in the broth, and green beans.
- Place a lid on the wok if possible then let the mix simmer for 6 mins. Add in the beef and soy sauce and cook the mix for 3 more mins.
- Enjoy.

Serving: 4

Timing Information:

Preparation	Cooking	Total Time
10 m	20 m	30 m

Nutritional Information:

Calories	375 kcal
Fat	28.6 g
Carbohydrates	6.2g
Protein	23 g
Cholesterol	76 mg
Sodium	139 mg

* Percent Daily Values are based on a 2,000 calorie diet.

Authentic Vietnamese Vermicelli

Ingredients

- 1/4 C. white vinegar
- 1/4 C. fish sauce
- 2 tbsps white sugar
- 2 tbsps lime juice
- 1 clove garlic, minced
- 1/4 tsp red pepper flakes
- 1/2 tsp canola oil
- 2 tbsps chopped shallots
- 2 skewers
- 8 medium shrimp, with shells
- 1 (8 oz.) package rice vermicelli noodles
- 1 C. finely chopped lettuce
- 1 C. bean sprouts
- 1 English cucumber, cut into 2-inch matchsticks
- 1/4 C. finely chopped pickled carrots

- 1/4 C. finely chopped diakon radish
- 3 tbsps chopped cilantro
- 3 tbsps finely chopped Thai basil
- 3 tbsps chopped fresh mint
- 1/4 C. crushed peanuts

Directions

- Get a bowl, combine: pepper flakes, vinegar, garlic, fish sauce, lime juice, and sugar. Let this mix sit on the side.
- Now begin to stir fry your shallots in veggie oil for 9 mins.
- Get your grill hot and coat the grate with oil.
- Stake 4 pieces of shrimp onto skewers then grill them for 3 mins per side. Then remove the shrimp from the grill.
- Begin to boil your vermicelli in water for 13 mins then remove all the liquids and run the noodles under some cold water.

- Evenly divide the following between serving bowls: shallots, vermicelli, lettuce, peanuts, bean sprouts, mint, Thai basil, cucumbers, cilantro, carrots, and daikon. Serve everything with a shrimp kabob and some of the lime sauce from the 1st bowl.
- Add some sauce to the serving and stir it.
- Enjoy.

Serving: 2

Timing Information:

Preparation	Cooking	Total Time
35 m	25 m	1 h

Nutritional Information:

Calories	659 kcal
Fat	12.8 g
Carbohydrates	112.3g
Protein	26.2 g
Cholesterol	36 mg
Sodium	2565 mg

* Percent Daily Values are based on a 2,000 calorie diet.

BAMBOO TOFU

Ingredients

- 2 tbsps white sugar
- 3 tbsps soy sauce
- 1 C. dry white wine
- 1/2 C. chicken broth
- 1 (14 oz.) package tofu, drained
- salt and pepper to taste
- 1 tbsp cornstarch
- 3 C. oil for frying, or as needed
- 1 onion, chopped
- 4 plum tomatoes, sliced into thin wedges
- 12 oz. fresh green beans, trimmed and cut into 3 inch pieces
- 1 C. bamboo shoots, drained and sliced
- 1 C. chicken broth, or as needed
- 2 tbsps cornstarch
- 3 tbsps water

Directions

- Get a bowl, combine: 1/2 C. broth, white sugar, white wine, and soy sauce.
- Drain and dry your tofu then dice it into cubes. Top the tofu with some pepper and salt then coat everything with 1 tbsp of cornstarch.
- Get about 1 in. of oil hot in a wok then deep fry the tofu in the oil until it is golden.
- Place the tofu to the side on some paper towels.
- In a 2nd frying pan get 1 tbsp of oil hot then begin to stir fry your green beans and onions for 6 mins then add some pepper and salt.
- Add in your tomatoes and cook them for 5 mins then add the bamboo shoots.
- Now combine in the sauce and beans and get everything boiling.
- Let the mix boil for 7 mins while stirring. Add some more broth (1 C.) if all the liquid cooks out.

- Combine in the rest of the cornstarch (2 tbsp) with water until smooth then add it to the mix.
- Stir and simmer everything until the mix is thick then add the tofu.
- Enjoy.

Serving: 4

Timing Information:

Preparation	Cooking	Total Time
20 m	20 m	40 m

Nutritional Information:

Calories	380 kcal
Fat	21.6 g
Carbohydrates	28.2g
Protein	11.7 g
Cholesterol	0 mg
Sodium	796 mg

* Percent Daily Values are based on a 2,000 calorie diet.

Radish Mushroom Sandwich

Ingredients

- 2 portobello mushroom caps, sliced
- 2 tsps olive oil
- salt and pepper to taste
- 1 carrot, sliced into sticks
- 1 daikon (white) radish, sliced into sticks
- 1 C. rice vinegar
- 1/2 C. fresh lime juice
- 1/2 C. cold water
- 1/2 C. chilled lime juice
- 2 tsps soy sauce
- 1 tsp nuoc mam (see recipe)
- 1/2 tsp toasted sesame oil
- 2 tbsps canola oil
- 2 tsps minced garlic
- 1/3 C. white sugar
- 1/3 C. cold water
- 1 jalapeno pepper, thinly sliced

- 8 sprigs fresh cilantro with stems
- 1 medium cucumber, sliced into thin strips
- 2 sprigs fresh Thai basil
- 2 (7 inch) French bread baguettes, split lengthwise

Directions

- Set your oven to 450 degrees before doing anything else.
- Top your mushrooms with olive oil, pepper, and salt. Lay out the mushrooms on a cookie sheet and toast them in the oven for 30 mins. Then let the veggies cool and julienne them.
- Now get a large pot of water boiling. Once the water is boiling get a bowl and fill it with ice water.
- Drop your radishes and carrots in the boiling water for about 20 secs then dump the veggies into the ice water.

- Get a 2nd bowl, combine: 1/2 C. cool fresh water, rice vinegar, and 1/2 C. of lime juice.
- Now submerge your radishes and carrots in this mix for 20 mins.
- Get a 3rd bowl, combine: 1/3 C. of water, the rest of the lime juice, 1/3 C. sugar, soy sauce, canola, sesame oil, and fish sauce.
- Coat the bread with the sauce then lay your roasted mushrooms on the bottom portion of the sandwich then top the veggies with more sauce, add some pieces of jalapeno, cilantro, sticks of carrots and radishes (no liquid), basil, and cucumbers.
- Enjoy.

Serving: 2

Timing Information:

Preparation	Cooking	Total Time
20 m	25 m	45 m

Nutritional Information:

Calories	760 kcal
Fat	22.8 g
Carbohydrates	128.4g
Protein	19.5 g
Cholesterol	0 mg
Sodium	1282 mg

* Percent Daily Values are based on a 2,000 calorie diet.

Nem Ran Hay Cha Gio

(Vietnamese Spring Rolls)

Ingredients

- 2 oz. dried thin rice noodles
- 3/4 C. ground chicken
- 1/4 C. shrimp - washed, peeled, and cut into small pieces
- 2 large eggs, beaten
- 1 carrot, grated
- 4 wood fungus mushrooms, chopped
- 2 green onions, chopped
- 1/2 tsp white sugar
- 1/2 tsp salt
- 1/2 tsp ground black pepper
- 24 rice paper wrappers
- 2 C. vegetable oil for frying

Directions

- Let your noodles sit submerged in water for 30 mins then remove all the liquids and dice the noodles into 3 inch pieces.
- Get a bowl, combine: green onions, noodles, mushrooms, chicken, carrots, shrimp, and eggs.
- Add in the black pepper, salt, and sugar then stir the mix.
- Submerge 1 wrapper in some water then layer 1 tbsp of mix in the middle.
- Roll up the edges of the wrapper and tightly to form a nice spring roll.
- Continue with the rest of the wrappers and ingredients.
- Fry your rolls, 3 at a time, in oil for 6 mins until golden.
- Enjoy.

Serving: 12

Timing Information:

Preparation	Cooking	Total Time
1 h	5 m	1 h 25 m

Nutritional Information:

Calories	132 kcal
Fat	5.2 g
Carbohydrates	14.4g
Protein	6.5 g
Cholesterol	45 mg
Sodium	225 mg

* Percent Daily Values are based on a 2,000 calorie diet.

Southeast Asian Chicken Breasts

Ingredients

- 1 tbsp vegetable oil
- 1 small yellow onion, chopped
- 1 (8 oz.) package baby bella mushrooms, chopped
- 4 cloves garlic, minced
- 8 C. water
- 1 (6.75 oz.) package rice stick noodles (such as Maifun(R))
- 8 tsps chicken bouillon
- 2 cooked chicken breasts, shredded
- 4 green onions, chopped
- 1/3 C. chopped fresh cilantro
- 2 C. bean sprouts
- 1 lime, sliced into wedges
- 1 dash Sriracha hot sauce, or more to taste

Directions

- Stir fry your garlic, mushrooms, and onions for 8 mins then combine in the bouillon, noodles, and water.
- Get everything boiling then set the heat to low.
- Combine in the cilantro, green onions, and chicken.
- Let the mix cook for 8 more mins then divide the soup between serving bowls.
- When serving the soup top it with some sriracha, bean sprouts, and lime juice.
- Enjoy.

Serving: 6

Timing Information:

Preparation	Cooking	Total Time
15 m	15 m	30 m

Nutritional Information:

Calories	231 kcal
Fat	5.4 g
Carbohydrates	32g
Protein	13.5 g
Cholesterol	28 mg
Sodium	149 mg

* Percent Daily Values are based on a 2,000 calorie diet.

Chicken and Rice Soup

Ingredients

- 1/8 C. uncooked jasmine rice
- 1 (2.5 lb) whole chicken
- 3 (2 inch) pieces fresh ginger root
- 1 stalk lemon grass, chopped
- 1 tbsp salt, or to taste
- 1/4 C. chopped cilantro
- 1/8 C. chopped fresh chives
- ground black pepper to taste
- 1 lime, cut into 8 wedges

Directions

- Get the following boiling in a large pot: salt, chicken, lemon grass, water, and ginger.
- Once the mix is boiling place a lid on the pot, set the heat to low, and let the contents gently cook for 90 mins.

- Now run the contents through a strainer and place the chicken to the side and the liquid back in the pot. Remove the bones and skin from the chicken and dice the meat into small pieces.
- Add the rice to the broth and get everything boiling. Once the mix is boiling set the heat to medium and cook the mix for 35 mins.
- Add the rice to a bowl and add the chicken, pepper, chives, and cilantro on top.
- Cover everything with lime juice.
- Enjoy.

Serving: 4

Timing Information:

Preparation	Cooking	Total Time
10 m	2 h	2 h 10 m

Nutritional Information:

Calories	642 kcal
Fat	42.3 g
Carbohydrates	9.8g
Protein	53 g
Cholesterol	1210 mg
Sodium	1943 mg

* Percent Daily Values are based on a 2,000 calorie diet.

Shrimp Cucumber Sandwich

Ingredients

- 1 large carrot, peeled and shredded
- 1 stalk celery, chopped
- 2 scallions (green onions), chopped
- 1/4 C. rice vinegar
- 1/3 C. chopped fresh cilantro
- 3 tbsps low-fat mayonnaise
- 3 tbsps low-fat plain yogurt
- 1 tbsp lime juice
- 1/8 tsp cayenne pepper
- 3 (12 inch) French baguettes, cut into halves
- 1 lb frozen cooked prawns, thawed and tails removed
- 18 thin slices cucumber, or more to taste

Directions

- Get a bowl, combine: scallions, carrots, and celery. Top the mix with the vinegar and stir everything.
- Now get a 2nd bowl, combine: cayenne, cilantro, lime juice, yogurt, and mayo.
- Coat one side of your bread with 2 tbsp of mayo sauce then layer the veggies on top of the sauce.
- Add the prawns to the rest of the yogurt mix and layer them on top of the veggies in the sandwich.
- Add a final layer of cucumber then form a sandwich with the other piece of bread.
- Cut the sandwich into 6 pieces and serve.
- Enjoy.

Serving: 6

Timing Information:

Preparation	Cooking	Total Time
	20 m	20 m

Nutritional Information:

Calories	388 kcal
Fat	3.3 g
Carbohydrates	60.9g
Protein	28.2 g
Cholesterol	148 mg
Sodium	886 mg

* Percent Daily Values are based on a 2,000 calorie diet.

Nuoc Cham

(Vietnamese Beef Sauce)

Ingredients

- 2 cloves garlic, minced
- 1 tsp crushed red pepper flakes
- 3 tbsps white sugar
- 2 tbsps lime juice
- 4 tbsps fish sauce
- 1 C. water

Directions

- Get a bowl, combine: water, garlic, fish sauce, red pepper flakes, lime juice, and sugar.
- Mix everything together until it is smooth and serve the sauce over cooked beef.
- Enjoy.

Serving: 6

Timing Information:

Preparation	Cooking	Total Time
	5 m	5 m

Nutritional Information:

Calories	32 kcal
Fat	0.1 g
Carbohydrates	< 7.6g
Protein	0.6 g
Cholesterol	0 mg
Sodium	730 mg

* Percent Daily Values are based on a 2,000 calorie diet.

Bo Luc Lac with Asian Vinaigrette

(Garlic Sirloin)

Ingredients

Beef Marinade:

- 2 tbsps minced garlic
- 2 tbsps oyster sauce
- 1 1/2 tbsps white sugar
- 1 tbsp fish sauce
- 1 tbsp sesame oil
- 1 tbsp soy sauce
- 1 tsp hoisin sauce
- 1 1/2 lbs beef top sirloin, cut into 1-inch cubes

Vinaigrette:

- 1/2 C. rice vinegar
- 1 1/2 tbsps white sugar

- 1 1/2 tsps salt
- 1 red onion, thinly sliced

Dipping Sauce:

- 1 lime, juiced
- 1/2 tsp salt
- 1/2 tsp ground black pepper
- 2 tbsps cooking oil
- 2 bunches watercress, torn
- 2 tomatoes, thinly sliced

Directions

- Get a bowl, combine: hoisin, garlic, soy sauce, oyster sauce, sesame oil, 1.5 tbsp sugar, and fish sauce.
- Stir the mix until it is smooth then add in the beef. Stir the meat then place a covering of plastic on the bowl and put everything in the fridge for 60 mins.

- Get a 2nd bowl, combine: onions, vinegar, 1.2 tsp salt, and 1.5 tbsp sugar.
- Stir the mix until it is smooth then place it in the fridge for 13 mins.
- Now get a 3rd bowl, combine: black pepper, lime juice, and 1/2 tsp salt. Place the sauce in some ramekins for dipping later.
- Begin to stir your beef in hot oil, in a wok.
- Brown the beef in batches for 3 mins then stir everything for 3 more mins until done.
- Add a layer of watercress on a platter for serving then add the tomatoes, top the veggies with the vinaigrette.
- Now add your beef and place the onions in 2nd bowl for serving over everything.
- Enjoy with the ramekins of sauce.

Serving: 6

Timing Information:

Preparation	Cooking	Total Time
30 m	5 m	1 h 35 m

Nutritional Information:

Calories	292 kcal
Fat	17.4 g
Carbohydrates	13.3g
Protein	21.7 g
Cholesterol	60 mg
Sodium	1238 mg

* Percent Daily Values are based on a 2,000 calorie diet.

Bo Luc Lac II

(Garlic Tenderloin)

Ingredients

- 1 1/2 lbs beef tenderloin, cut into cubes

Marinade:

- 2 tbsps olive oil
- 2 tbsps oyster sauce (such as Maekrua(R))
- 4 large cloves garlic, minced, or more to taste
- 1 tbsp Cabernet Sauvignon wine
- 1 tsp fish sauce
- 1 tsp ground black pepper, or more to taste
- 1 tsp soy sauce (optional)
- 1 tsp dark soy sauce (optional)
- 2 drops sesame oil, or more to taste

Dipping Sauce:

- 1 tbsp fish sauce (optional)
- 1 tbsp lemon juice (optional)
- 1 tbsp ground black pepper (optional)
- 2 tbsps olive oil
- 2 tbsps oyster sauce
- 4 cloves garlic, minced, or more to taste

Directions

- Get a bowl combine: sesame oil, 2 tbsp olive oil, dark soy sauce, 2 tbsp oyster sauce, regular soy sauce, 4 minced garlic cloves, 1 tsp black pepper, wine, and 1 tsp fish sauce.
- Once the mix is smooth add in the beef and stir the meat to evenly coat everything.
- Now place a covering of plastic on the bowl and put everything in the fridge for 50 mins.
- Get a 2nd bowl, combine: 1 tbsp black pepper, 1 tbsp fish sauce,

and lemon juice. Combine the mix until it is smooth.
- Begin to stir fry your beef with marinade in 2 tbsp of hot olive oil for a few mins then add: 4 cloves of garlic, and 2 tbsp oyster sauce.
- Let the mix cook and simmer for 9 mins until it becomes thick.
- Now add your garlic one clove at time instead of all at once to get a better taste.
- Serve with the sauce in the 2nd bowl.
- Enjoy.

Serving: 6

Timing Information:

Preparation	Cooking	Total Time
30 m	5 m	45 m

Nutritional Information:

Calories	329 kcal
Fat	26.8 g
Carbohydrates	3.4g
Protein	17.7 g
Cholesterol	60 mg
Sodium	458 mg

* Percent Daily Values are based on a 2,000 calorie diet.

Lemongrass Chicken

Ingredients

- 2 tbsps canola oil
- 2 tbsps finely chopped lemongrass
- 1 tbsp lemon juice
- 2 tsps soy sauce
- 2 tsps light brown sugar
- 2 tsps minced garlic
- 1 tsp fish sauce
- 1 1/2 lbs chicken thighs, or more to taste, pounded to an even thickness

Directions

- Get a bowl, combine: fish sauce, canola, garlic, lemongrass, brown sugar, lemon juice, and soy sauce. Once the sugar is fully incorporated combine in the

chicken and stir the contents to coat the meat.
- Place a covering of plastic around the dish and put everything in the fridge for 65 mins.
- Now get your grill hot and coat the grate with oil.
- Grill the meat for 4 mins per side until it is fully done.
- Enjoy.

Serving: 4

Timing Information:

Preparation	Cooking	Total Time
10 m	10 m	40 m

Nutritional Information:

Calories	308 kcal
Fat	19 g
Carbohydrates	3.9g
Protein	29 g
Cholesterol	105 mg
Sodium	339 mg

* Percent Daily Values are based on a 2,000 calorie diet.

Vietnamese Spring Rolls

Ingredients

- 1/4 C. white vinegar
- 1/4 C. fish sauce
- 2 tbsps white sugar
- 2 tbsps lime juice
- 1 clove garlic, minced
- 1/4 tsp red pepper flakes
- 2 oz. rice vermicelli
- 8 large shrimp, peeled and deveined
- 4 rice wrappers (8.5 inch diameter)
- 2 leaves lettuce, chopped
- 3 tbsps finely chopped fresh mint leaves
- 3 tbsps finely chopped cilantro
- 4 tsps finely chopped Thai basil

Directions

- Get a bowl, combine: pepper flakes, vinegar, garlic, fish sauce, lime juice, and sugar.
- Let your vermicelli sit submerged in warm water for 65 mins.
- Now boil your shrimp in fresh water and salt for 2 mins then place the shrimp to the side and cut them in half.
- Add the noodles to the boiling shrimp water and cook them for 2 mins also.
- Drain the liquid and rinse the noodles until cool water.
- Now dip a wrapper in some water then layer on it: 1/4 C. Thai basil, 4 pieces of shrimp, 1/4 C. cilantro, 1/4 C. lettuce, 1/4 C. mint, and 1/2 oz. of noodles.
- Shape the mix into an eggroll.
- Continue creating rolls in the manner until all the ingredients have been used up.
- Slice each roll into 2 pieces then top each with some fish sauce mix or place the mix to the side.
- Enjoy.

Serving: 4

Timing Information:

Preparation	Cooking	Total Time
20 m	5 m	1 h 25 m

Nutritional Information:

Calories	137 kcal
Fat	0.7 g
Carbohydrates	22.5g
Protein	10.1 g
Cholesterol	64 mg
Sodium	1170 mg

* Percent Daily Values are based on a 2,000 calorie diet.

Rice and Shrimp Salad

Ingredients

- 8 large fresh shrimp, peeled and deveined
- 3 tbsps olive oil
- 3 cloves garlic
- 1/2 C. fresh mint
- 1/4 C. chopped fresh cilantro
- 3 tbsps fish sauce
- 2 tbsps honey
- 1 lime, juiced
- 1/4 tsp ground white pepper
- 2 tbsps fresh ginger root, minced
- 3/4 C. shredded cabbage
- 1 (6.75 oz.) package dried rice noodles

Directions

- Get your grill hot and oil the grate.

- Puree the following in a food processor: white pepper, garlic, lime juice, 1/4 C. mint, honey, cilantro, and fish sauce.
- Now get a large sauce pan with water boiling then add the cabbage and noodles. Let the noodles cook for 4 mins.
- At the same time cover your shrimp with olive oil and grill the fish until they are fully done on both sides.
- Now dice the rest of the mint (1/4 C.) and place everything in a bowl with some sauce and noodles.
- Top the dish with some more mint.
- Enjoy.

Serving: 2

Timing Information:

Preparation	Cooking	Total Time
25 m	10 m	35 m

Nutritional Information:

Calories	565 kcal
Fat	21.3 g
Carbohydrates	85g
Protein	10 g
Cholesterol	44 mg
Sodium	1757 mg

* Percent Daily Values are based on a 2,000 calorie diet.

Pho IV

Ingredients

- 4 lbs beef soup bones
- 1 onion, unpeeled and cut in half
- 5 slices fresh ginger
- 1 tbsp salt
- 2 pods star anise
- 2 1/2 tbsps fish sauce
- 4 quarts water
- 1 (8 oz.) package dried rice noodles
- 1 1/2 lbs beef top sirloin, thinly sliced
- 1/2 C. chopped cilantro
- 1 tbsp chopped green onion
- 1 1/2 C. bean sprouts
- 1 bunch Thai basil
- 1 lime, cut into 4 wedges
- 1/4 C. hoisin sauce (optional)
- 1/4 C. chile-garlic sauce (such as Sriracha(R)) (optional)

Directions

- Set your oven to 425 degrees before doing anything else.
- Layer your beef bones on a cookie sheet and cook them for 65 mins in the oven.
- Now lay your onions on a cookie sheet as well and cook them in the oven alongside the beef for 50 mins.
- Add the following to a big saucepan: fish sauce, beef bones, star anise, onion, salt, and ginger.
- Add in 4 qts of water and get everything boiling. Once the mix is boiling set the heat to low and let the contents cook for 8 hrs.
- Now run the broth through a strainer and let it sit.
- Let your noodles sit submerged in water for 65 mins. Then get your stock boiling again.
- Evenly distribute your noodles between 4 bowls then top them with some green onions, cilantro, and sirloin.

- Add some boiling stock to each bowl, and cover the beef with the stock.
- Let the beef sit in the hot liquid for 4 mins until it is somewhat cooked and then add some sriracha, bean sprouts, lime wedges, and Thai basil to each bowl.
- Enjoy.

Serving: 4

Timing Information:

Preparation	Cooking	Total Time
20 m	8 h	9 h 20 m

Nutritional Information:

Calories	509 kcal
Fat	11 g
Carbohydrates	65.6g
Protein	34.9 g
Cholesterol	74 mg
Sodium	3519 mg

* Percent Daily Values are based on a 2,000 calorie diet.

Lime Cilantro Catfish

Ingredients

- 1/3 C. water
- 2 tbsps fish sauce
- 2 shallots, chopped
- 4 cloves garlic, minced
- 1 1/2 tsps ground black pepper
- 1/4 tsp red pepper flakes
- 1/3 C. water
- 1/3 C. white sugar
- 2 lbs catfish fillets
- 1/2 tsp white sugar
- 1 tbsp fresh lime juice
- 1 green onion, thinly sliced
- 1/2 C. chopped cilantro

Directions

- Get a bowl, combine: fish sauce, and 1/3 C. of water.

- Get a 2nd bowl, combine: pepper flakes, shallots, black pepper, and garlic.
- Now begin to stir and heat 1/3 C. of sugar and 1/3 C. of water until the mix turns caramel colored.
- Now add in the fish sauce mix then get everything boiling. Once the mix is boiling add your shallots and let them soften.
- Once the shallots are soft add the catfish, place a lid on the pot, and let the mix cook for 6 mins per side.
- Now remove your fish and it in a dish.
- Turn up the heat on the stove and stir in 1/2 tsp of sugar, lime juice, and any drippings from the fish in the dish.
- Get everything boiling, set the heat to low, and let the contents simmer until some of the sauce evaporates.
- Coat your fish with the sauce, some cilantro, and green onions.
- Enjoy.

Serving: 4

Timing Information:

Preparation	Cooking	Total Time
10 m	30 m	40 m

Nutritional Information:

Calories	404 kcal
Fat	17.4 g
Carbohydrates	24.1g
Protein	36.8 g
Cholesterol	107 mg
Sodium	676 mg

* Percent Daily Values are based on a 2,000 calorie diet.

Vietnamese Green Beans

Ingredients

- 1/2 tsp vegetable oil
- 1/2 yellow onion, chopped
- 1 tsp minced garlic
- 1 lb fresh green beans, trimmed and halved
- 1/4 C. soy sauce
- 3 tbsps nuoc mam (see recipe)
- 1/4 C. water
- 1 medium tomato, diced
- salt and pepper to taste

Directions

- Stir fry your shallots and onions in oil until they are soft then add the green beans.
- Stir the veggies then add the fish sauce and soy sauce.
- Let the dish cook for 4 mins while stirring.

- Add the water and get the mix gently boiling with high heat then a low to medium level of heat.
- Let the mix gently cook for 12 mins.
- Now add some pepper, salt, and the tomato.
- Enjoy.

Serving: 4

Timing Information:

Preparation	Cooking	Total Time
15 m	15 m	30 m

Nutritional Information:

Calories	64 kcal
Fat	0.8 g
Carbohydrates	12.4g
Protein	4.1 g
Cholesterol	0 mg
Sodium	1732 mg

* Percent Daily Values are based on a 2,000 calorie diet.

Hanoi Rice Noodle Spicy Salad

Ingredients

Dressing:

- 1/4 C. water, or more to taste
- 3 tbsps lime juice
- 3 tbsps fish sauce
- 3 tbsps brown sugar, or more to taste
- 1 clove garlic, minced
- 1 tsp minced fresh ginger root
- 1/2 tsp Sriracha chile sauce

Salad:

- 1 (8 oz.) package (linguine-width) rice noodles
- 2 C. thinly sliced Napa (Chinese) cabbage
- 1 1/2 C. matchstick-cut carrots

- 8 oz. grilled shrimp
- 1 C. bean sprouts
- 1/2 English cucumber, halved lengthwise and cut into thin slices
- 2 green onions, thinly sliced
- 2 2/3 tbsps chopped fresh mint
- 2 2/3 tbsps chopped fresh cilantro
- 2 2/3 tbsps chopped fresh basil
- 1/2 C. coarsely chopped peanuts

Directions

- Get a bowl, combine: sriracha, water, ginger, lime juice, garlic, and brown sugar.
- Once with sugar has been fully incorporated begin to boil a saucepan full of water.
- Once the water is boiling shut the heat and let your noodles sit submerged in the hot water for 5 mins.
- Stir the noodles to separate them.

- Now remove all the liquids and run the noodles under cold water.
- Place the noodles in a bowl with: basil, cabbage, cilantro, carrots, mint, shrimp, green onions, bean sprouts, and cucumber.
- Top the salad with your dressing then stir the mix.
- Add the peanuts as a topping.
- Enjoy.

Serving: 4

Timing Information:

Preparation	Cooking	Total Time
	25 m	30 m

Nutritional Information:

Calories	450 kcal
Fat	10.1 g
Carbohydrates	71g
Protein	20.4 g
Cholesterol	109 mg
Sodium	1265 mg

* Percent Daily Values are based on a 2,000 calorie diet.

A Vietnamese Drink

Ingredients

- 1 dragon fruit (pitaya)
- 2 tangerines, peeled and segmented
- 1 lime, juiced
- 4 leaves fresh basil
- 2 tbsps brown sugar
- 1 C. sparkling mineral water, chilled
- 1 C. crushed ice

Directions

- Take your dragon fruit and cut quarter inch pieces from it.
- Now puree the rest of the fruit with: sparkling water, tangerine, brown sugar, and basil. Once the mix is smooth add in the crushed ice and serve everything in a chilled glasses.

- Add the pieces of dragon fruit to the dish for decoration.
- Enjoy.

Serving: 2

Timing Information:

Preparation	Cooking	Total Time
	10 m	10 m

Nutritional Information:

Calories	149 kcal
Fat	0.8 g
Carbohydrates	40g
Protein	1.4 g
Cholesterol	0 mg
Sodium	9 mg

* Percent Daily Values are based on a 2,000 calorie diet.

Lemon Cabbage Lunch Vietnamese Style

Ingredients

- 1 head cabbage, cored and shredded
- 2 onions, halved and thinly sliced
- 2 C. shredded, cooked chicken breast
- 1/4 C. olive oil
- salt and pepper to taste
- 3 tbsps lemon juice, or to taste

Directions

- Get a bowl, combine: chicken, onions, and cabbage.
- Stir the mix then add in some olive oil and stir everything again.
- Now add: the lemon juice, pepper, and salt. Stir the mix again then place a covering of

plastic on the bowl. Put everything in the fridge for 5 hrs.
- Enjoy.

Serving: 6

Timing Information:

Preparation	Cooking	Total Time
	15 m	4 h 15 m

Nutritional Information:

Calories	231 kcal
Fat	12.7 g
Carbohydrates	15.5g
Protein	15.7 g
Cholesterol	35 mg
Sodium	66 mg

* Percent Daily Values are based on a 2,000 calorie diet.

Thanks for Reading! Now Let's Try some Sushi and Dump Dinners....

Send the Book!

To grab this **box set** simply follow the link mentioned above, or tap the book cover.

This will take you to a page where you can simply enter your email address and a PDF version of the **box set** will be emailed to you.

I hope you are ready for some serious cooking!

[Send the Book!](#)

You will also receive updates about all my new books when they are free.

Also don't forget to like and subscribe on the social networks. I love meeting my readers. Links to all my profiles are below so please click and connect :)

[Facebook](#)

[Twitter](#)

Come On...
Let's Be Friends :)

I adore my readers and love connecting with them socially. Please follow the links below so we can connect on Facebook, Twitter, and Google+.

Facebook

Twitter

I also have a blog that I regularly update for my readers so check it out below.

My Blog

Can I Ask A Favour?

If you found this book interesting, or have otherwise found any benefit in it. Then may I ask that you post a review of it on Amazon? Nothing excites me more than new reviews, especially reviews which suggest new topics for writing. I do read all reviews and I always factor feedback into my newer works.

So if you are willing to take ten minutes to write what you sincerely thought about this book then please visit our Amazon page and post your opinions.

Again thank you!

INTERESTED IN OTHER EASY COOKBOOKS?

Everything is easy! Check out my Amazon Author page for more great cookbooks:

For a complete listing of all my books please see my author page.

Printed in Poland
by Amazon Fulfillment
Poland Sp. z o.o., Wrocław